I0117458

Anonymous

The Royal Cook Book

Light Bearer's Circle of the King's Daughters

Anonymous

The Royal Cook Book
Light Bearer's Circle of the King's Daughters

ISBN/EAN: 9783744792448

Printed in Europe, USA, Canada, Australia, Japan

Cover: Foto ©Andreas Hilbeck / pixelio.de

More available books at **www.hansebooks.com**

The
Royal Cook Book

COMPILED BY

THE LIGHT BEARERS' CIRCLE

OF

THE KING'S DAUGHTERS

"She put forth a bill of fare that might kindle exhilaration in the heart of a misanthrope."—*Nicholas Nickleby.*

PUBLISHED BY
THE SILVER CROSS PUBLISHING CO.
158 WEST 23D STREET
NEW YORK CITY

Menus.

BREAKFAST.

Fruit.

Cocoa.   Coffee.

Codfish Balls.   Fricassee Chicken.

Creamed Potatoes.

Steamed Oatmeal.   Graham Gems.

Rice Griddle Cakes with Maple Syrup.

LUNCH.

Curry.   Saratoga Fried Potatoes.

Biscuits.   Chicken Croquettes.

Lemon Jelly.   Olives.

Cocoanut Cookies.   Banana Cake.

Tea.   Coffee.

"A good dinner brings out all the softer side of man."

DINNER.

Chicken Soup with Celery.

Veal Loaf.   Mint Sauce.

Baked Potatoes.   Sweet Potatoes.

Creamed Turnips.   Baked Tomatoes.

Spiced Currants.   Mixed Pickles.

Lemon Pie.   Tapioca Cream.

Ice Cream.

Sponge Cake.   Watermelon.   Cake.

Coffee and Whipped Cream.

"Good sister let us dine and never fret."

RECIPES.

Bread.

Three tablespoons flour, two of sugar, one of salt. Pour over about one quart of boiling water, and, when cool, add three yeast cakes, previously soaked in lukewarm water, and let rise. Then take one dozen or fifteen large potatoes, boil, mash and put through a colander with about three quarts of water alternating first hot then cold, until the potatoes are through the colander. When cool add the above; put in warm place and let rise. Then bottle up and keep in cool place. Three cups of the yeast will make two loaves of bread. In the morning mix yeast with flour and knead into a hard loaf and let rise. Then put into bread tins and let rise again before baking. As the yeast gets old add a very little soda at each time using. Bread to be nice and palatable should be kneaded a long time; the object of kneading the dough is to break all the bubbles of gas and make the bread fine grained; this work can be expedited by frequently slashing the dough with a sharp knife during the process of kneading.

WHITE BREAD.

Have ready two quarts sifted flour. Then prepare the mixing as follows. Take one quart of milk and scald. Stir in a piece of lard or butter the size of an egg and two tablespoonfuls sugar, also add salt. Set to cool until only milk warm. Dissolve cake of compressed yeast in a little

water and add to the above, and stir all into the flour.
Knead twenty minutes, cover with bread towel and let
rise. When it is sufficiently light, knead a little and make
into loaves and let rise again. Bake forty minutes.
Water may be used in place of milk.

WHITE BREAD.

Boil and mash fine six potatoes. Add to this half a cup
of flour and wet with boiling water from which the potatoes
were taken, stirring briskly until the ingredients are well
mixed. This batter should not be very thick when hot.
Set away to cool and when lukewarm add a yeast cake
(Twin Brothers preferred) dissolved in a little water.
Set in a warm place to rise. This sponge may be made
at noon and it will be light enough at tea time to use for
the bread sponge. Make a sponge of a quart of tepid
water, a piece of lard the size of an egg, salt and flour
to make a nice batter. Add the potato sponge which must
be of a frothy lightness, beat well and let rise. Knead into
bread before retiring. Knead again early in the morning
and put in tins. This bread dough makes delicious rolls.

BROWN BREAD.

One pint sour milk, one teaspoon soda, a little
molasses, thicken with Graham flour and a little corn
meal. Bake in a loaf.

CORN BREAD.

One cup sweet milk, one cup sour milk, one cup wheat
flour, one-half cup molasses, teaspoon soda, a little salt
and corn meal to make a batter of such thickness as may
be poured into a tin.

GERMAN BREAD.

One pint milk boiled, one half teacup sugar, two-thirds
teacup soft yeast, two tablespoonfuls lard. Make a rising
with the milk and yeast. When light put in the sugar
and shortening with flour enough to make as soft a
dough as can be handled. Flour the paste-board well, roll

out about half an inch thick. Put this quantity into two large pie tins, make a dozen indentures, with the finger, on the top, put small piece of butter in each, and sift over the whole one tablespoonful sugar mixed with one teaspoonful cinnamon. Let this stand until perfectly light. Bake in a quick oven fifteen or twenty minutes.

GRAHAM BREAD.

One quart white bread sponge, half a cup sugar, a little salt, stir in Graham flour until it is as stiff as can well be stirred with an iron spoon; put into a greased tin and let rise. Bake in a quick oven.

GRAHAM BREAD WITHOUT YEAST.

One cup sweet milk, one cup sour milk, one teaspoon soda, one half cup molasses, a little salt; stir in Graham flour to make a thick batter. Bake in a quick oven. This recipe may be used for Graham gems.

JOHNNY CAKE.

Small half cup sugar, a pinch of salt, two small cups sour cream or milk, one coffee cup Indian meal, one egg, one-half teaspoon soda, flour enough to make such consistency as can be poured into tin.

SUET JOHNNY CAKES.

One and one-half cups buttermilk or very sour milk, one teacup maple sugar, one-half cup flour, one teaspoon soda, a half teaspoon salt. Stir in a sufficient quantity of Indian meal to make a stiff batter and add a cup of chopped suet. Bake in a quick oven thirty minutes.

Rolls and Biscuits.

BAKING POWDER BISCUIT.

One quart flour before sifting. Put into it three teaspoonfuls baking powder; rub into the flour a piece of lard the size of an egg, add a little salt. Wet with water as soft as can be handled. Do not knead more than is necessary. Butter may be used. Have a very quick oven if you wish light biscuit.

CREAM BISCUIT.

One cup sour cream, one cup sweet milk, one teaspoon soda, one teaspoon cream of tartar, a small teaspoon salt. Stir in flour to make a dough. Mix as soft as can be handled, roll to a half inch in thickness, cut in round cakes and bake in a quick oven. Sour milk may be used in place of sweet by adding a little more soda.

PARKER HOUSE ROLLS.

Two quarts flour, one pint milk, one cup yeast, or one yeast cake dissolved in a little lukewarm water, four tablespoons melted lard, a little salt. Warm the milk and add lard, sugar, salt and half the flour. Mix this at nine o'clock in the morning. At twelve stir in the remainder of flour. At half-past threé roll about half an inch thick, cut and spread lightly with butter. Raise until twenty minutes of six. Bake in hot oven twenty minutes.

RUSKS.

One and one-half cups milk, one-half cup sugar, half a yeast cake dissolved in half cup water. Make a sponge. Let it rise over night. In the morning add half cup sugar, half cup butter, a little cinnamon and half teaspoon soda. Stir in flour enough to roll in the hands. Make in the shape of biscuit, place in tins and let rise.

Breakfast and Tea Dainties.

APPLE FRITTERS.

Three eggs beaten very light, one quart milk. Make a thin batter. Add a little salt and the grated rind of one lemon. Pare, core and slice thin one quart nice tart apples; add to the batter and drop by spoonfuls in boiling lard. Serve with maple syrup.

BUNS.

At noon take one cup warm, one cup cold water, one cup yeast, one cup sugar, and flour to make a batter about as thick as for griddle cakes. Let rise until night; then add one cup sugar, one cup butter, currants, salt and flour enough to knead. Let it rise until morning, then roll in small pieces and put in baking pans. Let them rise two or three hours. Bake in a quick oven.

CLAM FRITTERS.

Take raw clams, chopped fine. Make a batter with the liquor, an equal quantity of sweet milk, four eggs to each pint of liquid and flour sufficient to stiffen. Fry like other fritters.

CORN CAKE.

One pint sweet milk, one-half cup sugar, one-half cup butter, two cups meal, three cups flour, three eggs, two teaspoonfuls baking powder.

CORN MEAL MUSH.

Put two quarts water over the fire, salt to taste. When it boils stir in sifted corn meal by the handful, letting it sift through the fingers slowly. Stir rapidly all the while and keep batter boiling. When it becomes very stiff set on back of the stove and boil slowly a few minutes. Serve with syrup or cream and sugar. This is nice when cold, sliced, and fried in hot lard or butter.

CORN OYSTER CAKES.

One dozen medium sized ears of corn. Grate, add four eggs, yolks and whites beaten separately; a little salt;

beat corn and yolks thoroughly together; stir in the whites, stiffly beaten, very gently. Fry in half butter and half lard. Drop in the hot fat in quantity the size of a medium oyster.

CURRY.

Take cold meat—beef, veal or chicken, cut up in small pieces with one onion sliced thin. Put in water to cover it, and cook until very tender, then add a piece of butter, salt, curry to taste. Thicken with a small tablespoonful flour; last add the juice of one lemon. Serve with boiled rice.

GRAHAM GEMS.

One cup of hot water poured over three tablespoons of shortening. When melted, add one cup of sweet milk, a little salt, half a cup of sugar, two teaspoons baking powder, mixed with sufficient Graham flour to make a batter not very stiff. Let the gem irons be hot, put in batter and bake quickly.

GREEN CORN FRITTERS.

Take twelve ears of sweet corn, instead of grating, slit each row of kernels through the middle from end to end, and scrape out the pulp. Add three eggs, one teacup flour, one heaping teaspoonful baking powder, a little salt and pepper. If necessary add a little milk. Cook as pancakes over a hot griddle.

HOMINY MUFFINS.

To one cup well cooked hominy add one well beaten egg, three tablespoonfuls melted butter and two-thirds cup of milk. Stir into the mixture two cups of flour, into which has been sifted two teaspoonfuls baking powder. Mix and bake in muffin rings in a quick oven.

MOTHER'S MUFFINS.

One egg, one pint of sweet milk, a little salt, two table-spoons sweet cream, flour to make a batter which will drop from the spoon and not drip. Bake in muffin rings.

STEAMED OAT MEAL.

One half-pint oat meal, a teaspoon salt. Put in a two-quart basin and pour over it one quart boiling water; put in a steamer and steam two hours. Do not touch until done.

STRAWBERRY SHORTCAKE.

Use recipe for baking powder biscuit. Roll out into two cakes and spread first one with butter and then place over it the second; then bake quickly. When done open and put in berries. Whipped cream is nice with this.

STRAWBERRY SHORTCAKE.

One quart flour, one-half coffeecup butter rubbed into the flour, two teaspoonfuls of cream of tartar, one tea-spoonful soda, milk to make a soft dough. Roll out, mark off in squares with a knife, and bake in pie tins. When the cakes are taken from the oven split them with a sharp knife and butter them. Cover one-half with a layer of sugared berries mashed just enough to start the juice. Lay upon this another half and cover with berries as before. Proceed until the pile is complete. Cut in wedge shaped pieces and serve hot.

WAFFLES.

Two cups milk, three cups flour, two eggs, one tea-spoon cream of tartar, one-half teaspoon soda, one small pinch of salt and a tablespoonful melted butter. If this batter is too stiff, add melted butter. Bake in waffle irons.

Griddle Cakes.

"'Tis nought in making,
'Tis all in baking."

BREAD GRIDDLE CAKES.

Cover one pint of stale bread with cold water and let stand over night. In the morning mash very fine, add one pint sour milk, one teaspoon soda, one egg, a little salt and flour to make as stiff as ordinary batter cakes.

BUCKWHEAT CAKES.

Put two yeast cakes, previously soaked, into a pint of tepid water with wheat flour enough to make a stiff batter. When light put into a jar and add one quart warm water, a little salt and enough buckwheat flour to thicken it. In the morning thin the batter with sweet or sour milk, in which is dissolved a little soda if sweet milk and more soda if sour. The best thing for greasing the griddle is a piece of raw salt pork. The cakes must be turned as soon as they are a light brown on the under side, or as soon as bubbles form on the upper side.

FLAPJACKS.

One-half cup sour cream, one-half cup sour milk, one teaspoon soda, one egg, salt and flour to make a batter. The egg may be omitted. Sweet milk may be used with three teaspoons baking powder, one egg and a little shortening.

RICE GRIDDLE CAKES.

One cup cold boiled rice, one cup flour, a little salt, two eggs, milk to make a medium thick batter. Beat together and bake on a hot griddle.

Meats and Sauces.

FRICASSEE CHICKEN AND CHICKEN PIE.

If you have a large chicken and a small family, make a fricassee with plenty of rich, highly seasoned gravy. Break open hot baking powder biscuit and lay on a platter, lay on the neck, back, wings and part of the breast and pour over all plenty of gravy. This makes the first day's dinner. For the next dinner take what is reserved with any that is left, make more gravy by adding cream and butter, pepper and salt and a pinch of sugar; heat hot, line a baking dish with a crust made as you would baking powder biscuit; put in the chicken and bake.

FRIZZLED BEEF.

Put a piece of butter in a frying pan, then put in the beef and let it brown. Pour in hot water, put two table-spoonfuls of flour in a little milk, put in a beaten egg and boil up once.

OYSTER DRESSING.

Two quarts of bread crumbs, pour a little water over them, season with salt, pepper and butter and one pint of oysters, sage to taste.

SAUSAGE.

Ten pounds of pork, two ounces of salt, one ounce of black pepper, one-half ounce powdered sage, one grated nutmeg. One-third of the pork should be fat. The shoulder of the pig is the best to use.

SCALLOPED OYSTERS.

To one quart of oysters containing one-half cup of liquor, add in three layers one quart cracker crumbs, one-half cup of butter, three tablespoonfuls rich cream, a little salt and pepper.

VEAL LOAF. -

Three and one-half pounds of raw veal, chopped fine, six crackers, rolled fine, three raw eggs, a piece of butter size of an egg, a small slice of salt pork, a little salt and pepper. Mix in form of loaf and put bits of butter over it. Sprinkle rolled cracker over the top, and bake two hours, basting often.

SAUCES.

CAPER SAUCE.

Put one teaspoonful of butter in a frying pan to melt. Do not brown. Add one tablespoonful of flour. Stir until smooth. Now add one pint of broth in which the leg was boiled. Stir constantly until it boils and is smooth. Add two large spoonfuls of capers, salt and pepper to taste.

DRAWN BUTTER.

Put a cup of milk into a stew pan, let it heat to boiling. Work a tablespoonful of flour into half a teacup of butter, pour over it a cup of boiling water. When smooth add it to the boiling milk, let it simmer five minutes.

FISH SAUCE.

Heat a cup of vinegar, stir into it half a cup of butter and a teaspoonful of made mustard, with a little pepper.

MINT SAUCE.

Chop a bunch of fresh mint, mix with a teaspoonful of sugar, and vinegar to moisten. Serve with roast lamb.

PARSLEY SAUCE.

Dip a bunch of parsley into boiling water, cut it fine and stir it into drawn butter.

Fish.

BAKED FISH.

Wash and dry the fish, spread it out in a dripping pan, the skin side down. Cover with thin slices of salt pork and put a little vinegar in the bottom of the pan. Bake until thoroughly done.

BOILED FISH.

Wring a cloth from hot water, flour it well, wrap it about the fish, and place it in the boiling water. Boil gently, allowing ten to fifteen minutes for each pound of fish. Serve with sauce.

CODFISH BALLS.

One pint of codfish, one pint of mashed potatoes, mix well with one egg, one teaspoonful butter and pepper to taste. With a large fork beat mixture light, make in small balls, dip into beaten egg and cracker crumbs and fry in butter.

SCALLOPED FISH.

Two pounds fresh cod, boiled day before using. Flake fine with fork. One cup grated bread. Place fish and bread in layers; season with salt and pepper. Pour milk or cream over dish and sprinkle with cracker crumbs. Bake in hot oven one-half hour.

Croquettes.

CROQUETTES.

One pint chopped meat, one pint bread crumbs, one onion, two eggs. Season with salt and pepper. Have quite moist and make in thin cakes. Fry in butter.

CHICKEN CROQUETTES.

Three cups of chopped chicken, one cup of soft bread crumbs, two eggs, pepper and salt to taste. Mix well together and form into pear-shaped balls. A little chopped parsley may be added. Roll them in egg, then in cracker, and fry in lard in a wire basket as dough-nuts.

FISH CROQUETTES.

Take cold fish of any kind, separate from the bone and chop fine. Add a little seasoning, an egg, a very little milk and a teaspoon of flour. Brush with an egg, roll in bread crumbs and fry in hot lard.

LOBSTER CROQUETTES.

To the meat of a well boiled lobster, chopped fine, add pepper, salt and powdered mace. Mix with this one-fourth as much bread crumbs, well rubbed, as you have meat; make into balls with two tablespoonfuls melted butter. Roll this in beaten egg, then in pulverized cracker and fry in butter, and garnish with crisp parsley.

Soups.

BEAN SOUP.

Soak one quart of dried beans over night. In the morning add a quart of cold water and set them where they will keep warm without boiling for one hour. Add the liquor in which pork has been boiled, add two chopped onions, four stalks of celery cut fine; strain, season with pepper, put it back in the kettle, let it boil, stir in one tablespoonful butter rolled in flour, simmer five minutes and serve.

CLAM CHOWDER.

Twenty-five clams, one-half pound of salt pork chopped fine, six potatoes sliced thin, four onions sliced thin. Put pork in kettle. After cooking a short time add potatoes, onions and juice of clams. Cook two and one-half hours, then add clams fifteen minutes before serving. Add two quarts of milk if desired.

CHICKEN SOUP.

A delicious chicken soup is made by cutting up one chicken and putting it in your kettle with nearly two quarts of water, a teaspoonful of salt and a little pepper. When about half done add two teaspoonfuls of barley or rice. When this is done remove the chicken from the soup, tear or cut part of the breast into small pieces and add to the soup with a cup of cream. The rest of the chicken may be reserved for salad or for chicken croquettes.

TURKEY SOUP.

Take the skeleton of a turkey after the meat has been cut from it, boil it in two quarts of water until the meat falls from the bone, strain, and add two tablespoonfuls rice. Season with pepper and salt and serve.

LAMB SOUP.

Boil a stew piece of lamb, take out the meat, strain the liquor, season, add green peas and new potatoes, cook until they are soft.

TOMATO SOUP.

Pare and slice four tomatoes, put in one pint boiling water, add one teacup of milk, pepper and salt, one-half teaspoonful soda, let it boil fifteen minutes, put in a little butter. Serve with crackers.

VEGETABLE SOUP.

Take the strained soup liquor, add one cup each of cabbage, turnips and potatoes, chopped (not too fine); cook thirty minutes, season with pepper, and serve. Onions may be added to suit the taste.

Vegetables and Salads.

BAKED TOMATOES.

Wash large smooth ripe tomatoes, cut piece from stem end about size of twenty-five cent piece, put in a pinch of salt, a little pepper and a small piece of butter. Set them in a tin and bake them in a moderate oven three quarters of an hour.

BOSTON BAKED BEANS.

Soak about three pints beans, from noon until night. Then put into bean pot with small piece of pork scored, add a little pepper and fill pot with water, put into oven at night and bake until next day noon.

CAULIFLOWER.

Cut off the stalk, boil the cauliflower in milk and water until it is tender, serve hot with bits of butter and a sprinkling of pepper and salt. It may be boiled in clear water with a little salt.

CORN FRITTERS.

One-half teacup butter, one-half teacup flour, one egg, pepper and salt, one pint grated corn. Beat it up, and fry it on a well buttered griddle. They are as good as fried oysters.

CREAMED TURNIPS.

Boil the turnips, when done turn off water, and cut into small pieces. Then stir a little flour into milk, season with butter, pepper and salt, and stir with the boiled turnips.

DEVILED TOMATOES.

Remove the seeds of large, ripe tomatoes, and fill up with chopped cold boiled veal, well seasoned with butter, pepper and salt, mixed with egg to make a stiff batter. Bake three quarters of an hour.

FRIED ONIONS.

Cut some pork into small pieces and fry in spider until crisp and brown. Then slice the onions and place in the hot fat a little pepper, and a very little water. Cover and cook slowly about one hour until done.

SARATOGA FRIED POTATOES.

Pare and slice potatoes very thin. Drop them in cold water, drain on a cloth, fry a few at a time in a good quantity of hot lard, stir gently, skim out, put in a colander to drain and sprinkle with salt.

SCALLOPED POTATOES.

Butter a baking dish, pare potatoes and slice thin, put in dish a layer of potatoes, sprinkle with salt, pepper, butter and a little flour, then another layer of potatoes, etc., until the dish is nearly full. Then fill with milk or cream. Bake one hour and a half. Put pieces of salt pork on the top of scalloped potatoes before put in the oven. This adds greatly to the flavor.

SCALLOPED VEGETABLE OYSTERS.

Boil until soft and mash fine; add salt, pepper and butter to taste, and a little milk. Mix together well and place in baking dish. Cover the top with bread crumbs with here and there a lump of butter. Bake a delicate brown.

STEWED CORN.

Scald the corn just enough to harden. Slice off ears so as to divide the kernal three or four times. Scrape the chits (the sweetest part) from the cob, add sweet milk, a little water, a little butter, and salt. Simmer ten minutes. Beat one egg and add, stirring it evenly, just before taking off the fire. A little sugar improves it for the taste of most people.

SALADS.

DRESSING FOR CABBAGE.

For one quart of finely chopped cabbage, two teaspoons melted butter, one teaspoonful mustard, one teaspoon sugar a little salt, one-half teacup vinegar. Yolks of two eggs, well beaten. Have the vinegar boiling hot before adding the other ingredients. Do not cook any time after the ingredients have been added to the vinegar. Mix thoroughly with the cabbage, add the beaten whites of two eggs as a finish for the salad.

MAYONNAISE DRESSING.

Yolk of one egg, mustard and cayenne pepper to taste. Stir these together, add olive oil, slowly stirring constantly until it is thick. Add a third of a teaspoonful of vinegar or a little lemon juice. Beat the white of an egg and stir into the dressing.

POTATO SALAD.

Boil a quart of potatoes, and when cold, cut in small pieces. Mix two onions with them and pour over a dressing, made of one-half cup cream, one-half cup vinegar, a piece of butter the size of an egg and two eggs.

The dressing should be cooked until thick as cream, and after it has cooled add salt, pepper and mustard.

POTATO SALAD.

One quart of warm boiled potatoes, three hard-boiled eggs; one onion chopped fine; yolks of two raw eggs; one-half cup melted butter. Stir potatoes, boiled eggs and onions together. Add salt and pepper to taste. Pour melted butter on yolks of raw eggs; stir until cool. Place on ice to cool. It will appear like wax. Just before using add two tablespoons sugar and one pint of chopped lettuce, also add one-half cup sweet cream.

SALMON SALAD.

Take one can salmon, pick over carefully with fork to remove all bones, then add an equal quantity of chopped celery; over this pour your salad dressing. Chicken salad may be made in the same manner as salmon salad.

TOMATO SALAD.

One peck of ripe tomatoes, eight small onions. Slice tomatoes and onions and put in a jar, with half a cup of salt. Let stand over night and then drain. Then add two quarts vinegar, one and one-half teaspoons cinnamon, one-half teaspoonful cayenne pepper, one-half pound of white mustard seed, one cup of sugar. Boil all together until onions are tender; then can them.

Cakes.

PLAIN CAKES.

CREAM CAKE.

Put two eggs in a teacup and fill with sweet cream. Add one cup sugar, one and one-half cups flour, one teaspoonful baking powder and a pinch of salt.

EASY CAKE

One cup sugar, one-half cup butter, two cups flour. Take one egg and break into a teacup and then fill the cup with sweet milk, two teaspoonfuls baking powder. Put into a dish and beat altogether. This is excellent for larger cakes.

FEATHER CAKE.

One cup sugar well beaten with three teaspoons butter, one-half cup milk, one egg, one and three-fourths cups flour, and one and one-half teaspoons baking powder. Add the grated rind of one lemon in place of extract.

DELICATE CAKES.

ANGEL CAKE.

White of nine large fresh eggs, one and one-fourth cups granulated sugar, one cup sifted flour, one-half teaspoon cream of tartar, a pinch of salt added to two eggs before beating. Sift flour several times before measuring. Sift and measure sugar. Beat whites of eggs about half, then add cream of tartar and beat until very stiff; stir in sugar, then flour very lightly. Put in pan and in a moderate oven at once. Bake from thirty-five to forty minutes.

CHOCOLATE CAKE.

One and one-half cups sugar, one-half cup butter, one-half cup sweet milk, three eggs. Dissolve ten teaspoonfuls of grated chocolate and three of sugar in two teaspoonfuls boiling milk. Add this to the first mixture together with one and three-fourths cups of flour, and one and one-half teaspoonfuls of baking powder. Bake in loaf or layers as desired.

CHOCOLATE LOAF.

One-half cup butter, two cups sugar, two cups flour, one-half cup coffee (hot), one-fourth cup of milk, two teaspoonfuls baking powder, two teaspoonfuls vanilla, two eggs and one square chocolate. Rub the butter and sugar to a cream and add the beaten eggs and then the milk. Grate the chocolate and add to the coffee, which should be very hot; stir well and gradually add this mixture to the butter, sugar and eggs; add the flour and baking powder, beating well. Then add vanilla. Bake in a loaf for forty minutes in a moderate oven.

COCOANUT LOAF.

One cupful sugar, one cupful milk, one-fourth cupful cocoanut, two cupfuls flour, one egg, two teaspoonfuls baking powder, three tablespoonfuls melted butter.

CORN STARCH CAKE.

Two cups fine white sugar, one cup butter, one cup sweet milk, one cup corn starch, two cups flour, white of five eggs, one-half teaspoonful soda dissolved in milk, one teaspoonful cream of tartar. Flavor with lemon.

DELICATE CAKE.

One cup sugar, small half cup butter, half cup sweet milk, whites of three eggs beaten stiff, two cups flour, one and one-half teaspoonfuls baking powder, one teaspoon lemon. Bake slowly. This is nice cut in squares frosted, and on each square place the half of an English walnut. Whipped cream is also nice, served with this, cut in squares.

GOLD CAKE.

Yolk of eight eggs, one cup of granulated sugar, scant one-half cup butter, one-half cup sweet milk, one and one-half cups flour, two teaspoonfuls baking powder. Bake in a moderate oven.

ONE TWO THREE WHITE CAKE.

Two cups sugar, one cup water, three cups flour, one-half cup butter, whites of three eggs and two teapoonfuls baking powder. For gold cake use same recipe, but use yolks in place of whites.

SPONGE CAKE.

Beat four eggs together very light, both yolks and whites. Then beat in two cups white sugar, granulated preferred; then one cup sifted flour, a little at a time; then another cup of flour in which two teaspoonfuls baking powder have been mixed; lastly a small teacup hot water, almost boiling. Do not put it all in at once, but pour in gradually. When making for the first time, one will be tempted to put in more flour, it is so thin. Do not do it, or your cake will be lost. Bake in shallow tins in a moderate oven. Lemon is a delicate flavoring for sponge cakes.

SPONGE CAKE.

One cup sugar, three eggs, yolks and whites beaten separately, one cup flour, one teaspoon baking powder, three tablespoons sweet milk.

WATER-MELON CAKE.

One cup sugar, one-half cup butter, one-half cup milk, whites of three eggs, added last, two cups of flour. Flavor to taste. Take about a third and color with confectioner's pink sugar or cochineal syrup and add currants or raisins to represent seeds. Put a layer of white at top and bottom and the pink in the middle. Bake as a loaf-cake.

WHITE POUND CAKE.

One teacup fine white sugar, one-half cup butter. Beat butter and sugar twenty minutes. Whites of two eggs, one teaspoon cream of tartar, one-half teaspoon soda, one-half cup sweet milk, two cups of flour. Flavor with lemon.

LAYER CAKES.

LAYER CAKE FOR ALL FILLINGS.

One cup of sugar, one cup sweet milk, two cups flour, one egg, three tablespoons melted butter, two teaspoons baking powder.

BANANA CAKE.

Two cups sugar, one-half cup butter, one cup milk, whites of four eggs, two and a half teaspoons baking powder, three cups flour. For the filling use the whites of three eggs mixed with sugar to make a soft frosting. Spread the layers with the frosting and cover with sliced banana.

CARAMEL CAKE.

One cup sugar, one-fourth cup butter, one-half cup milk, one-half cup grated chocolate, one cup flour (before sifting), two eggs, one teaspoon baking powder. Steam chocolate, stir in and bake in two tins. Caramel for filling: one-third cup milk, one cup sugar, butter the size of an egg. Boil one-half hour or until it feathers. Remove to a cold place and stir until cold before flavoring with vanilla. Do not put on cake until both are cold.

LEMON CAKE.

One cup sugar, one-fourth cup butter, one-half cup milk, three cups flour, whites of two eggs and yolk of one, two teaspoons baking powder. For filling use the juice and grated rind of one lemon, one heaping tablespoon flour, one cup sugar, yolks of two eggs, and two thirds of a cup of boiling water. Beat sugar and eggs together and add to the other ingredients. Cook, until thick as custard, in a double boiler or the top of a tea kettle. Use the remaining white of an egg for frosting.

MARBLE CAKE.

Whites of four eggs, one cup sugar, one-half cup butter, one-quarter cup sweet milk, two cups flour, one-half teaspoon soda, one teaspoon cream of tartar.   For dark part use yolks of four eggs, one cup brown sugar, one cup molasses, one-half cup butter, one-half cup sour cream, one tablespoon each of cinnamon, cloves and allspice, a little nutmeg, one-half teaspoon soda dissolved in cream. Drop alternately to cloud, first white, then dark.   Bake in a moderate oven.

ORANGE LAYER CAKE.

Two cups sugar, a small half cup butter, one cup sweet milk, three eggs, two large teaspoons baking powder, three cups of flour.   Bake in layers.   For filling use juice of one orange, yolk of one egg and thicken with confectioner's sugar,   Place pieces of sliced orange between layers with the filling.

ROLL JELLY CAKE.

Three eggs beaten hard, one cup sugar, one cup flour, one teaspoon baking powder.

CREAM PUFFS.

One cup hot water, one-half cup butter.   Boil together and while boiling stir in one cup dry sifted flour.   Take from the stove and stir to a smooth paste.   After this cools stir in three eggs not beaten.   Stir it five minutes. Drop in tablespoonfuls on a greased tin and bake in a hot oven thirty-five minutes.   Do not open door any oftener than necessary and do not let them touch each other. Cool on a paper as soon as possible so they will not sweat.

FILLING—One pint milk, two eggs, one-half cup flour, sugar to taste.   Cook and stir well.   Flavor with vanilla. When both are cool open sides of puffs and fill with cream.

CAKE FILLINGS AND FROSTING.

CREAM FILLING.

Two eggs, one pint milk, one-half cup flour, one-half cup sugar, one teaspoon vanilla.   Cook until thick.

CHOCOLATE FILLING.

One and one-half cups granulated sugar, about one-half cup water. Let boil. Then pour one-fourth cup boiling water into it and boil again to prevent graining. One-half square Baker's chocolate, grated, white of one egg; add chocolate last thing before taking from stove. Have white of the egg beaten stiff and pour syrup over it, and beat all together until cool.

FIG FILLING.

One pound figs. Dissolve about half a cup of sugar in water enough to cover it; chop the figs fine and stir into the sugar. They must be moist, but if too moist, drain off surplus water.

WHIPPED CREAM,

Flavored with vanilla and sweetened with pulverized sugar, makes nice filling for cake in cool weather.

BOILED ICING.

One cup granulated sugar, five tablespoonfuls water. Let boil until it feathers or threads from the spoon. When ready have white of one egg beaten stiff, and pour syrup over it. Stir until cool; then add either lemon or vanilla.

FRUIT CAKES.

ADA'S FAVORITE SPICE CAKE.

One cup brown sugar, one-half cup butter, two eggs, one cup milk, two and one-half cups of flour, three even teaspoonfuls baking powder, from one-half to three-fourths of a cup of seeded raisins, chopped fine, one heaping teaspoonful of cinnamon, one-half teaspoonful of nutmeg. Other spices may be added according to taste.

BREAD CAKE.

Two cups light bread-dough, one and one-half cup sugar, one-half cup butter, two eggs, one teaspoon soda, one cup raisins. Put in a dish, make a hollow in centre, and put all ingredients therein. Mix with the hand until smooth. Bake immediately.

BUTTERNUT CAKE.

One cup sugar, one-half cup butter, one-half cup sweet milk, one egg, one-half teaspoonful soda, one teaspoon cream of tartar, mixed with flour, two cups flour, three-fourths of a cup of seeded raisins, one cup of butternut or hickorynut meats; spice to taste.

COFFEE CAKE.

One cup sugar, one-half cup butter, one-half cup molasses, one egg, two and one-half cups of flour, one teaspoonful soda, two-thirds of a cup of ice-cold strong coffee; cinnamon, cloves and allspice to taste; one-half cup of raisins.

EGGLESS CAKE.

One cup sugar, heaping teaspoon of butter, one teaspoon cinnamon, one-half teaspoon cloves, one-half teaspoon allspice, one-half teaspoon vanilla, a little nutmeg, one teaspoon soda, a pinch of baking powder, one cup thick sour milk, two cups flour, one cup of fruit.

FEATHER CAKE.

One cup butter, even full; five eggs, white and yolks beaten separately; two cups of pulverized sugar, three cups of flour, one cup sweet milk, two teaspoonfuls baking powder, one pound English currants, one pound chopped raisins.

FRUIT CAKE.

One pound sugar, with three-fourths of a pound of butter, yolks and whites of ten eggs, beaten separately, one pound sifted flour, two pounds of raisins, two pounds of currants, one pound of citron, one-fourth pound candied lemonpeel, one teaspoon each of cloves, cinnamon and allspice, one-half cup molasses, one cup coffee, one teaspoon cream of tartar, one-fourth teaspoon of soda; add one cup of flour. Bake in a four-quart pan.

SPICE CAKE.

One cup of butter, two cups of sugar, three cups of flour, one cup of milk, one-half cup raisins, two eggs, one teaspoon of baking powder. Bake one hour in a moderate oven; add spice to taste.

MOLASSES CAKES.

GINGER BREAD.

One cup molasses, one-half cup hot water, one-half cup butter or lard, one-half teaspoon of ginger, one-half teaspoon soda, one egg, two cups flour.

MOLASSES FRUIT CAKE.

One and one-half cups of molasses, one and one-half cups of sugar, one and one-half cups of buttermilk or sour milk, one cup of butter, four cups of flour, two teaspoons of soda, one pound of raisins, one-half pound currants, one-half pound figs, cinnamon and spice to taste.

SOFT GINGER BREAD.

One and one-half cups molasses, one-half cup of brown sugar, one-half cup butter, one-half cup sweet milk, teaspoon of soda, teaspoon of all-spice, half teaspoon of ginger. Mix all together, add three cups of flour and bake in shallow pans.

COOKIES AND DOUGHNUTS.

COCOANUT COOKIES.

One and one-half cups butter, two and one-half cups sugar, one cup milk, two cups shreded cocoanut, two teaspoons baking powder, three eggs, yolks and whites beaten separately.

FRUIT DROPS.

Two eggs, one cup molasses, one cup sugar, two-thirds of a cup shortening, two-thirds of a cup buttermilk or sour milk, one-half cup chopped and seeded raisins, one-half cup English currants, four cups flour, one teaspoonful soda, one teaspoonful each of cloves, allspice and cinnamon. Drop on buttered pan and bake.

HERMETS.

Two cups sugar, one-half cup cold water, one cup finely chopped raisins, one egg, one teaspoonful each of soda, cloves and cinnamon. Roll thin and bake quickly.

MOLASSES COOKIES.

Two cups molasses, one cup shortening, two-thirds cup of hot water, two teaspoonfuls of soda, cinnamon and ginger to taste. When cool add flour enough to roll out.

MOTHER'S COOKIES.

One and one-half cups sugar, one cup butter, three eggs, one tablespoonful sweet milk, one teaspoonful soda. Make quite stiff with flour; roll out and bake.

ONE YEAR COOKIES.

One cup full each of sugar, butter and molasses, four cups flour, spice and ginger.

SUGAR COOKIES.

One cup butter, two cups sugar, one cup milk, two eggs, a little nutmeg, three teaspoonfuls of baking powder. Flour to roll out soft.

DOUGHNUTS.

One cup sugar, shortening the size of a butternut, one egg, one coffee cup sweet milk, a little salt, cinnamon, two teaspoonfuls baking powder. Add flour and fry in hot lard.

Desserts and Sauces.

BANANAS AND WHIPPED CREAM.

A very delightful and easily prepared desert is one of bananas and whipped cream. Cut bananas into small slices, and over this pour cream, beaten till very stiff. Do not sweeten cream till after it is whipped, and then use pulverized sugar. Flavor. Five bananas and one pint cream will make ample desert for six people. Serve in colored dish. Eat as soon as possible.

CORN STARCH BLANC MANGE.

One pint milk, two eggs, two teaspoons corn starch, four teaspoons sugar. Flavor to taste. Save out whites of eggs and make merangue.

CUSTARD BLANC MANGE.

Make a custard of one quart milk, four eggs, leaving out whites of two eggs; add large cup sugar as soon as taken from fire; pour it upon one ounce of gelatine, previously soaked in a little cold water. Whip remaining whites to a stiff froth, and beat into the custard till thoroughly mixed. Flavor with vanilla and pour into a mould.

FLOATING ISLAND.

Separate the whites of three eggs from the yolks, add to the whites one tablespoonful of white sugar; beat to a froth. Take one quart milk, let it come to a boil. When boiling, drop in the beaten whites about the size of an egg. When done skim them out on a plate. Add to the boiling milk the beaten yolks, then one tablespoon of corn starch, with sugar to sweeten, dissolved in a little cold milk. When cold, pour into a dish and slide the islands on top. Flavor with lemon or vanilla.

SOUR APPLES, BAKED.

Dig out the cores of nice, large, sour apples, set in long tins. Fill up the holes in apples with sugar and a small piece of butter, add a little water to keep apples from scorching. This is nicely served with whipped cream.

SPANISH CREAM.

One-third of a box of gelatine, soaked in one and one-half pint of milk. Boil, then stir in the beaten yolks of three eggs, add three tablespoons of sugar, then boil again. Beat the whites to a stiff froth, and stir in after taking the cream from the fire. Cool slowly.

TAPIOCA CREAM.

One quart milk, one cup sugar, one tablespoon corn starch, yolks of three eggs, three tablespoons tapioca, pinch of salt, and one teaspoon vanilla.

Let tapioca soak in two-thirds of a bowl of water three hours. Let one pint of milk come to a boil, add salt and tapioca. Then, after three or four minutes' boiling, add other ingredients, well beaten, except the other pint of milk. Let this boil for a few minutes, and then add remainder of milk, letting it cook until it thickens like cream. Then add whites of eggs, beaten for puff, and let brown in oven.

ICE CREAMS.

ICE CREAM.

One quart milk, one pint cream, one cup sugar, yolks of three eggs, beat yolks well, stir them with the milk, add the cream and sugar. Stir constantly until it is boiling hot. Cool, flavor and freeze.

ICE CREAM, WITHOUT EGGS.

Boil one quart of cream, sweeten and flavor to taste. When cool, freeze.

POOR MAN'S ICE CREAM.

For one quart milk use four to six eggs, according to size, one cup sugar, two teaspoons flavoring. Scald the milk, beat eggs and sugar together thoroughly, and stir into milk briskly. Strain, heat gradually until it begins to thicken. Cool, add flavoring, then freeze. Keep constantly in motion while freezing. Cream, to be fine, should be strained through cheesecloth two or three times.

PIES.

PIE CRUST.

Rub thoroughly three cups flour, one-half teaspoon salt, one cup lard, moisten with one-half cup water. Handle with knife as little as possible.

CREAM RAISIN PIE.

One coffee cup sugar, one coffee cup sweet cream, one-half cup raisins, yolks of two eggs, one tablespoon flour. Line a tin with crust, fill with the above and bake. Whites of two eggs and two tablespoons sugar for puff.

COCOANUT PIE.

One cocoanut grated, one quart milk heated to boiling and poured over the grated nut, two tablespoons butter, four eggs, sugar to taste. This makes two pies.

CREAM PIE.

One pint milk, put in pail in a kettle of hot water, one-half cup sugar, a little salt when near boiling, add one tablespoon corn starch and yolks two eggs dissolved in a little milk. When like cream, place in a baked crust. Beat whites of eggs well, add two tablespoons sugar. Spread and brown lightly.

LEMON PIE.

Grate the rind and squeeze the juice of one lemon. One cup of sugar, one cup cold water, yolks of two eggs stirred in sugar, one cup of flour wet to a paste with water, a little piece of butter and a little salt. Stir all together and cook in a double boiler until thick. Bake crust and pour in custard. Beat the whites of two eggs to a froth, add a tablespoon of sugar, put in oven and brown.

MOCK MINCE PIE.

One cup bread crumbs, two cups cold water, one cup brown sugar, one-half cup molasses, one cup chopped raisins, one-half cup vinegar, two tablespoons melted butter, one teaspoon each cloves, cinnamon and allspice.

ORANGE PIE.

Juice and grated rind of two oranges, four eggs, four tablespoons sugar, one tablespoon butter. Cream the butter and sugar, add beaten yolk of eggs, then the oranges, and lastly the whites beaten stiff and mixed in lightly. Bake with under crust.

PEACH PIE.

Fill a crust with peaches, canned or fresh. Sprinkle on flour. Add sugar to taste and bake without upper crust. Add the beaten whites of two eggs, when baked, and brown.

PUMPKIN PIE.

One quart sifted pumpkin, three pints of milk, one egg, or flour may be used in place of the egg, one and one-half cups sugar. Add cinnamon, ginger and all-spice to taste. Add a little salt. Bake two hours and a half.

PUDDINGS.

BAKED INDIAN PUDDING.

One quart milk, two heaping teaspoons of Indian meal, four of sugar, one of butter, three eggs, one teaspoon salt. Boil the milk in double boiler, sprinkle meal in it, stirring all the time, and cook twelve minutes, stirring often. Beat together eggs, salt, sugar and half a teaspoon of ginger. Stir the butter into the meal and milk. Pour this gradually on the egg mixture. Bake slowly one hour.

BLACK PUDDING.

One cup molasses, one cup flour, one-half cup cold water, one egg, one teaspoon soda. Steam one hour. Serve with sauce.

CHOCOLATE PUDDING.

Let one pint of milk come to the boiling point, add one-half cup sugar, three tablespoonfuls grated chocolate, one tablespoon corn starch. Boil until it thickens. Pour into molds and cool. Serve with sauce.

FRUIT PUDDINGS.

Line a deep dish with a crust, double the thickness of an ordinary pie crust, made in the same manner as for baking powder biscuit. Fill half full of fruit, black raspberries preferable. Sprinkle with sugar and bake without upper crust. While baking prepare a cream same as for cream pie recipe. When baked fill dish with cream prepared. Then add whites of two eggs beaten stiff and brown in oven.

FRUIT PUFFS.

One quart flour, three tablespoonfuls baking powder, add enough water to make a stiff batter. Add a little salt. Fill the buttered cups with a layer of batter, then add about two tablespoons of fruit, and then a layer of batter, enough to fill cups two-thirds full. Steam one-half hour. Serve with sauce.

GRAHAM PUDDING.

One-half cup molasses, one-fourth cup butter, one-half cup sour milk, one and one-half cups Graham flour, one cup raisins, one egg, one teaspoon soda. Spice to taste. Steam three hours.

ORANGE PUDDING.

Peel and cut up four large oranges, place in the bottom of a dish. Make and pour over them a custard, made of one quart of milk, one cup sugar, two tablespoons corn starch, yolks of four eggs. Make frosting of the whites, one-third of a cup of sugar. Spread over the top. Brown a little and serve cold.

RICE PUDDING (EXCELLENT).

Five even tablespoonfuls rice, ten tablespoonfuls sugar, cinnamon to taste. Put in a two-quart basin, and fill with milk. Bake three hours, stirring occasionally. Add raisins just broken open, if desired.

SNOW PUDDING.

One pint of milk, put on stove in double boiler. As soon as it boils have ready two large tablespoonfuls of corn starch, mixed with a little cold milk, and stir into the boiling milk. Flavor with lemon. When cooked, pour over the white of an egg, well beaten, and let cool.

CREAM FOR THE ABOVE.—One pint of milk, as soon as it boils add one-half cup sugar, the yolk of one egg, and one teaspoon of corn starch; flavor with vanilla. Let cool, and pour over the above when served.

SPONGE PUDDING.

Yolks of three eggs, four tablespoonfuls flour, one and one-half pint of milk, little salt. Stir milk scalding hot into flour, then add yolks, well beaten. When ready to put in oven add whites beaten to a froth. Bake one-half hour. Serve immediately.

STEAMED INDIAN PUDDING.

Two cups sweet milk, two cups meal, one cup flour, one cup dried cherries, two tablespoonfuls molasses, one teaspoon soda, two eggs. Steam two hours.

SWEET PUDDING.

One cup suet, one cup molasses, one cup sweet milk, three cups flour, one cup raisins, one teaspoonful soda. Steam two hours. Serve with sauce.

SAUCES.

FRUIT SAUCE.

Cherries, strawberries and plums strained, and the juice boiled and thickened with a little corn starch and sweetened, make good pudding sauces.

HARD SAUCE.

One cup granulated sugar, one-half cup butter. Work to a cream and flavor with grated nutmeg.

LEMON SAUCE.

One cup sugar, one tablespoon flour, juice of one lemon, and two-thirds of a cup of boiling water. Let cook in the top of a teakettle or dish of water. When cooked and smooth, have ready the white of an egg, beaten stiff, and stir together. Fruit juices may be used in the place of lemon.

Pickles and Jellies.

CHILI SAUCE.

Eight large, ripe tomatoes, one and one-half onions, one and one-half green peppers, one tablespoonful salt, two sugar, four of vinegar. Boil three hours. Put up and seal.

CUCUMBER PICKLES.

Wash the cucumbers and cover well with boiling water for five successive mornings; then wipe them dry and place in a stone jar. Take one gallon best cider vinegar, one tablespoonful alum, three-fourths of a teacupful of coarse salt, one tablespoon white mustard, one-half teacup sliced horse radish. Boil all together, pour over the cucumbers, and cover them. These pickles will keep a year.

GREEN TOMATO SAUCE.

Two gallons green tomatoes, sliced thin; twelve good-sized onions, chopped; one quart vinegar, one quart sugar, two sweet peppers, two tablespoons ground mustard, one tablespoon allspice, one tablespoon cloves. Cook about two hours. Two tablespoons salt. It is better to seal.

HIGDOM.

One peck green tomatoes, four green peppers, six large onions, all chopped fine. Mix, with one cup salt and drain well. Boil twenty minutes in one quart water and two vinegar, and drain. Two pounds sugar, three pints vinegar, one-fourth pound white mustard seed, two tablespoons cinnamon, one tablespoonful cloves, one tablespoonful allspice, one-half tablespoonful ginger. Boil thirty minutes.

MIXED PICKLES.

Two heads of cauliflower, two hundred small cucumbers, fifty little onions, one good head of cabbage, one-half pint of nasturtium, two or three dozen half-grown cucumbers, pared and cut into pieces one inch thick; two heads celery. Put vegetables into salt water over night, drain, and put to soak in vinegar and water two days; drain, and mix in spices. Boil a gallon of vinegar with two pounds of white sugar, pour over while hot. Do this for three mornings, using same vinegar. One-half pound white mustard seed, one-quarter cup ground pepper, one-quarter cup of cinnamon, one-half cup tumeric powder. Before putting away mix one-half cup mustard with olive oil, and stir into it.

PICKLED FRUITS.

To seven pounds of fruit add three pounds of sugar, one pint vinegar, cloves, allspice, cinnamon; place spices in cloth bag and boil in syrup. Steam fruit until tender, then drop in the hot syrup and boil a little while; then take out and place in jar. Boil syrup down and pour over the fruit.

PICKLED ONIONS.

Soak in weak brine over night, then steam fifteen minutes; place in spiced hot vinegar, and seal in jars.

SWEET PICKLES.

Take eight pounds green tomatoes and chop fine, add four pounds brown sugar, and boil down three hours. Add one quart of vinegar, a teaspoon each of mace, cinnamon, and cloves; boil about fifteen minutes; let cool, and place in jars or other vessels. Try this recipe once and you will try it again.

JELLIES.

CURRANT CONSERVE.

Six pounds ripe currants, six pounds sugar, three pounds raisins, stoned and chopped, the juice and chopped rind of three oranges; boil all together one-half hour.

JELLY—FROM BERRIES, CURRANTS OR SMALL FRUIT.

Put fruit in pan and place over a kettle of boiling water until juice can be extracted, then strain through a cloth. Boil juice five minutes then add to each pint of juice one pound sugar, and let it just boil enough to melt sugar, then place in moulds. It is best to heat the sugar.

ORANGE AND LEMON JELLY.

Soak one-half box gelatine in a bowl half full of water, when well soaked add water enough to make a quart of liquid, put in a tin pail and set in a kettle of boiling water. Add a large coffee cup of sugar. Let boil one-half or three-quarters of an hour. Grate the rinds of three oranges and one lemon, put the gratings in a white flannel bag, then slice the lemons and oranges and line the bottom and sides of mould with them. When the gelatine is sufficiently boiled, turn it hot through the bag of rinds into the moulds.

RASPBERRY JELLY.

Take eight quarts of raspberries and four quarts of red currants. Extract the juice. For each pint of juice take one pint of sugar. Cook twenty minutes.

SPICED CURRANTS OR GOOSEBERRIES.

Four pounds sugar, seven pounds fruit, one pint vinegar, all kinds of spice. Cook until thick

Confectionery.

ICE CREAM CANDY.

One cup sugar, one-third cup of water, one-fourth teaspoonful cream of tartar, butter the size of an egg. Boil together fifteen minutes, not stirring until taken from the fire, when extract is added.

NUT CANDY.

Take a plate well buttered and spread on it about half a pint of hickory nut kernels. Take a pint of maple molasses, boil it till it becomes thick and try it by dropping some in cold water. When it hardens in the water pour it over the kernels and stir up quickly.

CHOCOLATE CARAMELS.

Two cups of brown sugar, one cup of molasses, one cup of cream or milk, one-half cup of butter, one-half pound of grated chocolate, two tablespoonfuls flour. Boil the molasses, butter, sugar and flour for fifteen minutes, stir the chocolate into the cream and pour in the boiling syrup, and boil till done. Before pouring it out on buttered plates, add a teaspoonful of vanilla, and as it cools crease it in small squares.

VANILLA TAFFY.

Two tablespoons of vinegar, four tablespoons of water, six tablespoons of sugar. Boil twenty minutes, then pour into a buttered plate.

CHOCOLATE CREAMS.

Two cups of granulated sugar, one-half cup of water, one-half cake of Baker's Chocolate. Boil the sugar and water together just five minutes after it begins to boil. Stir continually while boiling. Add extract of vanilla to taste. Roll into fifty balls size of a marble, when cool

enough to handle.   Dissolve the chocolate in steam.
Roll the balls in it and place on buttered paper.

MOLASSES CANDY.

Two cups of Orleans molasses, one cup of brown sugar,
butter the size of a walnut.   Boil twenty minutes.   When
done, add to the candy two teaspoonfuls of cream tartar,
one teaspoonful of soda, one tablespoonful of vinegar.
Let it stand until cool enough to pull.

COCOANUT CANDY.

Two teacupfuls of white sugar, one-half teacupful of
sweet cream, butter the size of a walnut.   Let it boil fifteen
minutes, then stir in as much cocoanut as you think best.
Flavor to taste.

BUTTER SCOTCH.

Three cups of brown sugar, three-fourths of a cup of
water, butter the size of a walnut, a pinch of soda.   Flavor
to taste.   Cook until it begins to harden when dripping
from the spoon; pour it out into buttered pans.   As it
cools mark off in squares with a knife dipped in water to
keep from sticking.   When wanted for eating, turn the
pan bottom side up, knock on it, and the candy will come
out without any trouble.

FRENCH CREAM.

These candies are made with 4X confectioner's sugar,
and can be made without boiling.   The sugar can be ob-
tained at any grocery.   French vanilla cream :—Break into
a bowl the white of one or more eggs, add to it an equal
quantity of cold water, then stir (do not beat) in the confectioner's sugar, until you have it stiff enough to mould
in shape with the fingers.   Flavor with vanilla.   After it is
formed into balls, cubes, or any other shape desired, lay
them upon sheets of waxed paper or upon plates, and set
aside to dry.   This is the foundation of all French cream.

PARISIAN CREAMS.

Make the French cream recipe and divide it into three parts; leaving one part white, color one part pink with a few drops of fruit coloring, and the third part brown with grated chocolate. Make a cake about half an inch thick of the white cream, which may be done by rolling on platter or marble slab. Take the pink in the same manner, and lay it upon the white; then chocolate in the same, pressing it all together; trim the edges smooth and cut in squares. Each layer may be flavored differently.

Coffee.

Take a tablespoon of fresh-ground coffee for every person, make it moist with the white of an egg and a little cold water. Stir well. Pour over as much boiling water as will be needed to fill the cups, allowing one cup of water for the coffee pot. Set it where it will simmer fifteen or twenty minutes. No more water must be added; fast boiling gives coffee a rank taste.

COFFEE WITHOUT EGGS.

Having a perfectly clean coffee pot, put in as much boiling water as will be required to fill the cups, adding another cup for the pot. Set it where it will keep hot without boiling. Lay carefully on the top of the water a tablespoonful of coffee for each person, cover, and let it alone for twenty minutes. At the end of the time pour off a little of the coffee into a cup. If it is clear as brandy, it is ready for the table. If not clear, pour the coffee back into the pot and let it stand a few minutes longer. This coffee should be served with cream and sugar or boiled milk.

Miscellaneous.

Put hot water on boiled meats and cold water on soups.

A sure cure for chapped hands is something greatly desired. Try this: Wet your hands in warm water, then rub them all over with corn meal. Do this twice; then in the water used to wash off the meal put a teaspoonful of pure glycerine.

To cure earache: Take a pinch of black pepper, put it on a piece of cotton batting dipped in sweet oil, and place it in the ear and tie a bandage around the head. It will give almost instant relief.

In stoning raisins pour boiling water on them, then pour it off quickly.

How to make furniture look new: Take three parts of sweet oil, one part spirits of turpentine, and mix them. Rub off the dust and apply the mixture with a flannel cloth.

Paste for scrapbooks: Put in plenty of alum; it will prevent moths and mice.

A poltice of tea leaves applied to small burns will give almost instant relief.

Hot alum water is the best insect destroyer known. Put the alum into hot water, let it boil until it is all dissolved, then apply the solution hot to all cracks, closets, bedsteads and other places where insects are found. There is no danger of poisoning the family, or destroying the property.

Always put the cream of tartar in the eggs in making cake.

A strong solution of oxalic acid will remove dry paint, after you have tried everything else without success. Try this.

Weights and Measures

SOLIDS.

Wheat Flour, - - - -	1 lb.	equals 1 qt.
Indian Meal, - - - -	1 lb. 2 oz.	" 1 qt
Butter, when soft, - - -	1 lb. 1 oz.	" 1 qt.
Loaf Sugar, - - - -	1 lb.	" 1 qt.
White Sugar - - - -	1 lb. 1 oz.	" 1 qt.
Brown Sugar, - - -	1 lb. 2 oz.	" 1 qt.
Eggs, - - - - -	10	" 1 lb.

LIQUIDS.

4 tablespoons, - - - -	equal ½ gill.
4 gills, - - - - -	" 1 pint.
2 pints, - - - - -	" 1 quart.
4 quarts, - - - - -	" 1 gallon.
60 drops, - - - - -	" 1 teaspoon.
4 teaspoons, - - - -	" 1 wine glass.
12 tablespoons, - - - -	" 1 teacup.

INDEX.

www.ingramcontent.com/pod-product-compliance
Lightning Source LLC
Chambersburg PA
CBHW021559270326
41931CB00009B/1287